MW00780357

Released!

DISCOVERY SERIES BIBLE STUDY
For individuals or groups

Without question, one of the defining characteristics of our time is the prevalence of addictions. The complexities and pressures of life drive us to look for solutions—but sometimes the things we had hoped would bring us solutions for the struggles of life become the greatest struggle of all—an addiction that we can't set aside or escape. To help us find our way back, biblical counselors Tim Jackson and Jeff Olson offer us understanding that is both compassionate and direct. There is a way out—even when we think we can't stop. We trust that this study will be a helpful step in that direction.

—*Bill Crowder*
Associate Teacher, RBC Ministries

This Discovery Series Bible Study is based on
When We Just Can't Stop: Overcoming Addiction (CB961),
one of the popular Discovery Series booklets from RBC Ministries.
Find out more about Discovery Series at
www.discoveryseries.org

Copyright © 2011 by Discovery House Publishers

Discovery House Publishers is affiliated with RBC Ministries,
Grand Rapids, Michigan.

Requests for permission to quote from this book should be directed to the
Permissions Department, Discovery House Publishers, PO Box 3566, Grand Rapids, MI 49501,
or contact us by e-mail at permissionsdept@dhp.org

Unless otherwise indicated, Scripture is taken from the New King James Version.
©1982, Thomas Nelson, Inc., Publishers. Used by permission. All rights reserved.

DISCOVERY HOUSE

P U B L I S H E R S®

Managing Editor: Dave Branon
Study Guide questions: Sim Kay Tee, Dave Branon
Graphic Design: Steve Gier

ISBN: 978-1-57293-525-9
Printed in the United States of America

11 12 13 14 15 /10 9 8 7 6 5 4 3 2 1

Table of Contents

How To Use

DISCOVERY SERIES BIBLE STUDIES

The Purpose

The Discovery Series Bible Study (DSBS) series provides assistance to pastors and lay leaders in guiding and teaching fellow Christians with lessons adapted from RBC Ministries Discovery Series booklets and supplemented from items taken from the pages of *Our Daily Bread.* The DSBS series uses the inductive study method to help Christians understand the Bible more clearly.

The Format

READ: Each DSBS book is divided into a series of lessons. For each lesson, you will read a few pages that will give you insight into one aspect of the overall study. Included in some studies will be FOCAL POINT and TIME OUT FOR THEOLOGY segments to help you think through the material. These can be used as discussion starters for group sessions.

RESPOND: At the end of the reading is a two-page STUDY GUIDE to help participants respond to and reflect on the subject. If you are the leader of a group study, ask each member to preview the STUDY GUIDE before the group gets together. Don't feel that you have to work your way through each question in the STUDY GUIDE; let the interest level of the participants dictate the flow of the discussion. The questions are designed for either group or individual study. Here are the parts of that guide:

MEMORY VERSE: A short Scripture passage that focuses your thinking on the biblical truth at hand and can be used for memorization. You might suggest memorization as a part of each meeting.

WARMING UP: A general interest question that can foster discussion (group) or contemplation (individual).

THINKING THROUGH: Questions that will help a group or a student interact with the reading. These questions help drive home the critical concepts of the book.

DIGGING IN: An inductive study of a related passage of Scripture, reminding the group or the student of the importance of Scripture as the final authority.

GOING FURTHER: A two-part wrap-up of the response: REFER suggests ways to compare the ideas of the lesson with teachings in other parts of the Bible. REFLECT challenges the group or the learner to apply the teaching in real life.

OUR DAILY BREAD: After most STUDY GUIDE sessions will be an *Our Daily Bread* article that relates to the topic. You can use this for further reflection or for an introduction to a time of prayer.

Go to the Leader's and User's Guide on page 56 for further suggestions about using the Discovery Series Bible Study.

A Complex Problem

The Variety Of Addiction

M *ary is obsessed with food.* For years she has binged and purged, sometimes 20 or more times a day. Her compulsive routine seems to have a life of its own.

Bill has a love his wife knows nothing about. As a curious teen he discovered *Playboy* and *Penthouse.* Fifteen years later, he finds the R-rated movie choices on his cable TV carrier irresistible. His computer gives him easy access to the pornography on the Internet.

Carla lost her sobriety to alcohol. She wasn't down at the local bar slugging down beers. She was a closet drinker. No one in her family suspected her problem. She drank only while her husband was at work and while the kids were at school. Nothing too serious, she thought, until she became pregnant again and tried to stop for the sake of the baby.

As these examples suggest, addictions are not limited to illegal, mood-altering substances. Mary is addicted to food. Bill is a slave to his own sexuality. Carla is controlled by a substance freely sold from the shelves of her family supermarket.

Addictions raise many questions. Are they moral weaknesses, diseases, habits, or sins? Are they physical dependencies or complicated spiritual cycles? What's needed for change? Is it medical treatment, family intervention, daily group accountability, or spiritual transformation? Can behaviors be changed quickly, or will recovery be the process of a lifetime? If our answer to these questions is yes, or at least maybe, we are being honest about the complexity of addiction.

In the following pages, we'll look at this complexity, and we'll focus on some of the more critical personal and spiritual dimensions of addiction.

> ■ **FOCAL POINT**
>
> Almost anything you can enjoy can become an addiction. And when you're addicted, nothing else matters as much as getting your next fix. The compulsive nature of addictions becomes all-consuming and eclipses any meaningful relationships with family or friends. The end result is an ever-deepening isolation and eventual self-destruction.

The Complexity Of Addiction

Defining An Addiction. An addiction is an enslaving, destructive dependency. Random House defines *addiction* as "the state of being enslaved to a habit or practice or to something that is psychologically or physically habit-forming, as narcotics, to such an extent that its cessation causes severe trauma."

Because a person can be physically predisposed to an addiction, and because of the likelihood of medical complications, addictions are often viewed as a disease. It would be a mistake, however, to think only in terms of the physical dimensions. Most addictions are also rooted in moral choices and spiritual needs.

● TIME OUT FOR THE CHURCH

The church is known in many circles for being judgmental and unwelcoming toward those who struggle with addictions. "Get a life" and "Just stop it" are some of the ways Christians have responded to pleas for help.

But that's not the way Jesus handled those caught in the grip of addictive struggles. Instead, He invited those who were in despair and being crushed by an overwhelming burden of shame, contempt, fear, and guilt to come to Him so He could provide rest for their weary souls (Matthew 11:28). Healthy churches are communities where struggling is expected and believers are equipped to struggle well together. This is where people really listen. They are available and approachable. Strugglers feel at home because the church is a place to belong and then to believe. And that belief builds a solid foundation for transformational living.

—www.helpformylife.org

■ FOCAL POINT: Pornography

Many men are keeping a secret that's destroying their honor and poisoning their relationships: It's pornography. Even Christian men, young and old, from all walks of life, are becoming hooked by the lure of pornography. Not all men who have looked at pornography are addicted to it, but many are. For help with this specific addiction, take a look at the booklet *When a Man's Eyes Wander* at **www.discoveryseries.org**.

What is most important is not whether we are predisposed to an enslaving habit but whether we are willing to do whatever it takes to bring this predisposed "diseased body," habit, or idol under the control of reason and faith.

How Widespread Are Addictions? According to an article in *Library Journal*, 45 million Americans attend 140 different kinds of weekly recovery groups. Another 100 million are trying to help those who are in recovery. In other words, half of us are either in recovery or helping someone who is. If the whole picture could be seen, however, far more of us than anyone has ever dreamed are captive to enslaving, destructive dependencies that are ruining us and our relationships.

What Can Be Addictive? In his book *Addiction And Grace,* Gerald May has compiled a list of 105 items to which many have become irresistibly attached. The vast majority are good things such as food, work, exercise, shopping, and prescription drugs. Let's look at some of the more common ones.

Drugs And Alcohol. Mood-altering chemicals account for some of our most obvious addictions. They create physical, emotional, and social dependence on artificially induced feelings. Some stimulants, ranging from cocaine to nicotine, produce an exhilaration that creates an illusion of well-being, power, adequacy, and control. Others cause hallucinations of pleasure or terror. Depressants, such as alcohol, can temporarily relieve our anxieties and our inhibitions.

Food. With food, some of us attempt to satisfy not only the natural needs of our bodies but also insatiable emotional and spiritual longings. The more we eat to feel better, the more our bodies work with our emotions to increase the demand. The cycle is addictive.

Attempts to reverse the effects of overeating can also be addictive. If we're anorexic, we starve ourselves. If we're bulimic, we indulge and then purge ourselves of what we have eaten by the misuse of laxatives or self-induced vomiting. By indulging or depriving ourselves, we fall unwittingly into another enslaving, destructive dependency.

Sexual Pleasure. Addiction to sexual pleasure may involve marital or extramarital heterosexual, same-sex, fetish, or pornographic obsessions. Sexaholism becomes evident when healthy desires for intimacy are channeled into behaviors that rob us of our self-respect, freedom, self-control, and opportunity for healthy sexual enjoyment.

Work. According to Genesis, God created us to work the land, rule the world, and help one another in the process. It is not surprising, therefore, that in a fallen world we have turned work itself into a slavemaster and a god. Much of our cultural drivenness focuses around our longing for significance through professional accomplishments. Workaholics are chronically absorbed in a continuous stream of tasks. Our sense of well-being is wrapped up in what we do. Attempts to break our obsession with work result in depression and feelings of failure.

Relationships. We can also develop an enslaving, destructive dependence on people. A form of relational idolatry occurs when we view another person as the source of our identity and well-being. Alone, we feel empty, unfulfilled, and helpless. When threatened with separation, we fight to cling to the other person at all costs, even to the harm of the one we claim to love.

Gambling. By playing the lottery, gambling at casinos or racetracks, or betting on point spreads of sporting events, some have become addicted to numbers games. Mounting losses and dreams of financial freedom fuel the need for "one more chance." For the moment, the damage already done to family, friends, and future is overridden by the adrenaline rush of one more gamble.

A Complex Problem

STUDY GUIDE

read pages 6-11

1

To understand what it means to have an addiction and what things are addictive.

MEMORY VERSE
Romans 7:15—
"For what I am doing, I do not understand. For what I will to do, that I do not practice; but what I hate, that I do."

Warming Up

How did Random House define what *addiction* means? Explain in your own words what an addiction is.

Thinking Through

1. Are addictions moral weaknesses, diseases, habits, or sins? Why? What is the exact nature of addictions?

2. The authors said that "most addictions are also rooted in moral choices and spiritual needs" (page 8). What do they mean? What spiritual needs are in view here ?

3. How and when do seemingly good things like food, work, and relationships become addictions? How do you prevent them from becoming addictive in your life?

Going Further

Refer

What do the following verses teach us about the nature of sin?

Genesis 4:7
Numbers 32:23
Psalm 51:2
James 4:17

1. In everyday terms, what is Paul talking about in verse 15? How does this kind of struggle occur in our lives?

2. What does Paul mean that the law is good (v. 16)? Isn't the law—the standards—what makes him feel bad when he sins?

3. Verses 21–25 describe the battle within. What is the good news at the end? How does that relate to our struggles with addictive behavior?

15 For what I am doing, I do not understand. For what I will to do, that I do not practice; but what I hate, that I do. 16 If, then, I do what I will not to do, I agree with the law that it is good. 17 But now, it is no longer I who do it, but sin that dwells in me. 18 For I know that in me (that is, in my flesh) nothing good dwells; for to will is present with me, but how to perform what is good I do not find. 19 For the good that I will to do, I do not do; but the evil I will not to do, that I practice. 20 Now if I do what I will not to do, it is no longer I who do it, but sin that dwells in me. 21 I find then a law, that evil is present with me, the one who wills to do good. 22 For I delight in the law of God according to the inward man. 23 But I see another law in my members, warring against the law of my mind, and bringing me into captivity to the law of sin which is in my members. 24 O wretched man that I am! Who will deliver me from this body of death? 25 I thank God—through Jesus Christ our Lord!

Prayer Time

Use the *Our Daily Bread* article on the next page as a guide for a devotional and meditation time relating to addictions.

Reflect

1. Is there anything in your life—even something good—that is threatening to become addictive?

2. What was surprising about the concepts presented in the introduction?

Too Much

A red fox squirrel eyed the ear of dried corn Cecil Whited had attached to a tree trunk. It was irresistible. So he pounced on his dinner and began eating. As Cecil watched, old "Red" ate row upon row right down to the last kernel. Many days and many corncobs later, he had become very fat.

One day Cecil found this corn-fed rodent dead under the tree. He figured "Red" had gotten so heavy that he fell from a high limb.

Overindulging can be a human problem too, but food isn't our only downfall. The dried corn that destroys us may be such addicting substances as alcohol and tobacco. Or such innocent-sounding activities as hobbies, sports, and work. Our problem comes when we lose self-control. To subtract an addiction from our lives, we must understand two things:

1. We are united with Christ in His death to sin and resurrection to new life (Romans 6:5–7).

2. God is at work in us (Philippians 2:13).

We must then put faith to work. Here's how: Admit we are helpless, confess our habit as sin, become accountable to another Christian, pray, and rely on God.

Confession, accountability, prayer, God's Word, and dependence on Christ make up rich soil in which the fruit of self-control can grow.

—*Dennis De Haan*

GALATIANS 5:22–23—

But the fruit of the Spirit is . . . self-control. Against such there is no law.

■ Read today's *Our Daily Bread* at **www.rbc.org/odb**

The
Marks of
Addiction

Five Telltale Signs

T hose who work with people caught in addictions identify at least five telltale signs, which when found together indicate the presence of an enslaving, destructive dependency.

1. Absorbing Focus. All addictions consume time, thought, and energy. They are not mere pastimes. They are obsessions and preoccupations that demand more and more from us.

2. Increasing Tolerance. The pattern of diminishing returns is also common. We need increasing amounts to maintain the same effect. Drug addicts need more crack to get the same high. Alcoholics need more alcohol to maintain the "buzz" that came so easily at first. The sex addict moves from soft- to hard-core pornography, or from normal marital relations to socially and biblically forbidden encounters.

3. Growing Denial. To protect the sacred moments of our pleasure, we deny that our "interest" is ruining us. Because there is so much to lose, we hide from others the extent of our enslavement. We convince ourselves that we can stop whenever we want. We learn to live in two worlds at the same time. We even believe our own stories. We become accomplished actors in front of others because of our fear of being found out.

4. Damaging Consequences. There is no such thing as a harmless addiction. All addictions are destructive to ourselves and those we love. Directly or indirectly, our obsessions can destroy our family and our friendships. We can lose our job, our health, our self-respect, and our reputation. Addictions are enslaving, destructive dependencies. They destroy our capacity for self-control and our ability to know and enjoy the God who has made us for himself.

5. Painful Withdrawal. Anything we habitually use to give us an artificial sense of well-being results in pain when it's taken away. Angry outbursts, agitation, anxiety, panic attacks, tremors, and depression are all costs of withdrawal. When deprived of our addiction, we are likely to feel that we have lost something essential to our survival.

In light of such painful results, we might wonder why we are so willing to become dependent on self-destructive ways of thinking and acting.

Why Do We Cling To Addictions?

Addictions are not just diversions of choice. We see them as lifeboats necessary for our survival. Addictions give us something we believe we must have in order to live. They provide predictable relief and power in an unpredictable and painful world.

The Pursuit Of Relief. When faced with a loss of health, when haunted by harm done to others, when hounded by the rejection of a parent or spouse, it is natural for us to try to relieve the pain. We hate feeling guilty, disconnected, empty, and alone. We long for acceptance and love. Our addictions provide a remedy that helps us to forget the pain—at least for a little while.

When do you know that you're addicted to something? Perhaps the central answer to that is this: When does whatever you're engaging in feel like anything but a choice? When it is not just a choice to enjoy. When it is a demand for a certain kind of pleasure, and you have to compromise any other commitment in order to achieve that kind of pleasure.

Alcoholism drowns sorrow. Drug addiction turns lows to highs. Compulsive overeating fills our emptiness. Obsessive work replaces insecurities with a sense of accomplishment. Sexual addiction mimics adventure and intimacy.

Addictions often begin as a pursuit of pleasure to numb the discomfort of painful losses. But we soon discover that addictions multiply the pain. In time, it becomes worse than the pain we were trying to relieve. Now we find ourselves needing relief not only from our inescapable losses but also from the shame of our own foolishness. We feel shame for trusting in addictive behavior that made our problem worse.

Shame, however, is also a deceiver. In the beginning, pleasure holds us in the addiction. In time, shame has the same effect. In their own ways, both are deceptively effective pain relievers. Pleasure is a filler; shame is a killer. Pleasure is a distracter; shame is an assassin. Both attach to our addictions. Both combine with our obsessions to numb our hearts not only to the harm we are doing to others but also to our own longing for love and relationship.

Ironically, shame ends up being even more useful than pleasure in providing relief from our pain. Shame causes us to feel unworthy to give and receive love. Shame deadens our longings for relationship. Shame becomes a powerful pain killer not merely by lessening our pain but by deadening our hearts until we feel nothing at all.

At the root of all disordered desires, there is really a spiritual element.

When our hearts are deadened, we don't hurt. We don't long to give and receive love. Neither are we able to feel the harm we are doing to others. Yet using our addiction and its resulting shame to feel nothing seems preferable to bearing the sorrows of life.

The Pursuit Of Power. Addictions also provide an illusion of control. They are like private magic carpets that transport us into a world where we seem to be in charge. They provide a predictable way of changing the way we feel about ourselves and others.

Addictions provide us with predictable moments we can count on, while giving us the illusion of control. While people and circumstances are beyond our control, our addictions deliver on their promise of comfort, pleasure, power, control—now. By refusing to eat, by purging what we have eaten, by using our work to attain recognition, by making another purchase, we feel power rather than helplessness.

Addictions are attractive because they appear to provide predictable doses of relief and power in the midst of pain and helplessness. But in reality they are a house of mirrors, promising us freedom and then trapping us with little hope of escape. The effect is always self-destructive bondage.

What we find out too late is that in exchange for relief and control, our addictions master us. Even though we tell ourselves we have everything under control, experience tells us otherwise. We'd quit if we could. But we have become a slave to our own desires.

We want our addiction more than we want to quit. We believe we need and deserve the relief and the power our addiction provides.

At some point, we are forced to choose between our addiction and those who love us. We know what we desperately want. We don't want to lose those we love. But we don't know how we could survive without the "friend" that is destroying us. We feel trapped in an addictive cycle.

What Is The Addictive Cycle?

As we lose more and more of ourselves to our addiction, our pleasure decreases. Moments of relief are replaced by lingering shame. We feel guilty for having a habit that is socially unacceptable. We are afraid of being discovered. In turn, we resolve to quit, or to make amends for our failures, hoping it will lessen our feelings of guilt and shame.

But it never does. We may have temporarily swept our lives clean of the addiction and its unpleasant feelings, but nothing has replaced it. As a result, we are more acutely aware of our emptiness. Feelings of disillusionment and despair set in, and once again we begin to demand relief. Our demand for relief draws us back into the familiar arms of our habit.

This cycle is played out again and again with deepening levels of dissatisfaction, disillusionment, despair, and enslavement.

2 The Marks of Addiction

STUDY GUIDE
read pages 15-19

To examine the signs of addiction and the reasons it creates such a destructive cycle.

MEMORY VERSE

2 Peter 2:19 (NIV)—
"They promise them freedom, while they themselves are slaves of depravity—for a man is a slave to whatever has mastered him."

Warming Up

What is the difference between preference and obsession, habit and addiction? When does a preference becomes an obsession and a habit becomes an addiction?

Thinking Through

1. What are the telltale signs of an addiction? Must all five marks be present before it is considered an "addiction"? Why or why not? What other signs would also be indicative of the presence of an addiction?

2. Why would you agree or disagree with the authors that "there is no such thing as a harmless addiction" (page 16)?

3. The authors say that we cling to our addictions because we see them as "lifeboats necessary for our survival" (page 16). What do they mean? Why are addictions necessary for our survival?

Going Further

Refer

What do the following verses tell us about the things of the flesh and the things of the Spirit?

Romans 7:5

Romans 8:9

2 Corinthians 3:6

Ephesians 6:12

Digging In   Read   Romans 8:5–9

1. What is the difference between the "things of the flesh" and the "things of the Spirit"? Discuss some things that fall into those two categories.

2. Why is the "carnal mind" not "subject to the law of God"? What does it mean to be "in the flesh"?

5 For those who live according to the flesh set their minds on the things of the flesh, but those who live according to the Spirit, the things of the Spirit. 6 For to be carnally minded is death, but to be spiritually minded is life and peace. 7 Because the carnal mind is enmity against God; for it is not subject to the law of God, nor indeed can be. 8 So then, those who are in the flesh cannot please God. 9 But you are not in the flesh but in the Spirit, if indeed the Spirit of God dwells in you. Now if anyone does not have the Spirit of Christ, he is not His.

3. How does the teaching in verse 9 relate to addictions to sinful practices? How does having the Spirit of God dwelling in a person help with addictions?

Prayer Time
Use the *Our Daily Bread* article on the next page as a guide for a devotional and meditation time relating to addictions.

Reflect

1. Do you see any of the marks of addiction showing up in any of the habits you find in your life?

2. What are the signs of a "deadened heart" as Tim Jackson and Jeff Olson describe it?

"Kill the Spider!"

As Christians, we sometimes have mixed feelings about our sins. We are afraid of being hurt by our sins, and we want to be forgiven. But we aren't sure we want to be rid of them right now.

A man told me he has a bad habit that is hindering his fellowship with God and hurting his Christian testimony. He says he prays that God will forgive him for his addiction—but he doesn't stop. He reminds me of the man in an old story who often went forward in church and knelt at the altar and prayed, "Lord, take the cobwebs out of my life." One Sunday morning his pastor, tired of hearing the same old prayer, knelt beside him and cried out, "Lord, kill the spider!"

Yes, sometimes it takes radical action to break a sinful habit. We need to do more than ask God for cleansing each time we succumb to temptation, important as that is. We must also ask God to help us take the necessary steps to keep the cobwebs out of our life. We must hate our sin, confess our bondage to it, and determine to be done with it. That's the principle behind Jesus' statement "if your right eye causes you to sin, pluck it out." Then we must feed our mind with good thoughts and stay away from the people and places associated with our sin.

Killing the spider gets rid of the cobwebs.

—Herb Vander Lugt

MATTHEW 5:29—

If your right eye causes you to sin, pluck it out and cast it from you.

■ Read today's *Our Daily Bread* at **www.rbc.org/odb**

What Does It Take To
Break the
Cycle? PART 1

A Spiritual
Dimension

S ometimes it takes family intervention to get our attention. It may take court-ordered treatment. Sometimes it takes financial ruin, loss of employment, loss of health, or loss of relationships.

Something must bring us to the end of ourselves. Something must cause us to be willing to reach out for whatever spiritual or medical help or daily accountability meetings we need to break the grip of our enslaving, destructive dependency.

One thing is certain. Even if hospitalization and medical treatment are needed to break the stranglehold of our addiction, we will need spiritual help to recover our sanity, sobriety, and self-control.

Addiction involves our spiritual inner being. We have needs that cannot be met by filling them with food, alcohol, drugs, or work. Physical obsessions cannot satisfy our deep longings for satisfaction, security, and significance.

Because these needs are spiritual rather than physical, most addiction treatment centers now recognize the need for more than medical or social therapy. Many programs are built around a form of spiritual treatment called 12-step recovery. Next we will consider some of the strengths and weaknesses of this approach.

The History of 12-Step Recovery

This is the widely adapted program of Alcoholics Anonymous. AA has it roots in the Oxford Group, which in the early part of the twentieth century encouraged spiritual renewal as a means of breaking the grip of alcoholism.

The Oxford Group was founded in 1908 when a YMCA secretary named Frank Buchman had a spiritual experience that reportedly changed his life. Published accounts indicate that in June of 1908 Frank started a streetside church in Philadelphia. The church flourished, and he started a hospice for young men that spread to other cities.

Before long, however, Frank had a violent argument with his trustee committee because they cut the budget and the food allotment. He resigned and went to Europe, ending up at a large religious convention in Keswick, England. His spiritual transformation occurred when he heard a speaker talk simply about the cross of Christ. He sensed the chasm separating him from Christ, and he felt the need to surrender his will. He went back to his house and wrote these words to each of his six trustees in Philadelphia: "My dear friend. I have nursed ill feelings against you. I am sorry. Will you forgive me? Sincerely, Frank."

Feeling an urge to share this experience, he went to nearby Oxford

⬛ FOCAL POINT: Can the church help?

True Christian fellowship within the local church involves submission to one another and admonishing, forgiving, and forbearing one another.

—Richard W. De Haan

University and formed an evangelical group there among the student leaders and athletes. In time, this group emphasized not only personal faith in Christ but also the need for the following:

1. Coming to the end of oneself

2. Others

3. Dependence on God

4. Self-examination

5. Confession of character defects

6. Restitution for harm done

7. Working with others

In 1934, members of the Oxford Group taught some of the principles of their fellowship to an alcoholic by the name of Ebby Thatcher, who was about to be locked up as a chronic drunk in Bennington, Vermont. Later, Ebby taught these principles to a childhood friend and fellow alcoholic named Bill Wilson. Wilson later became a co-founder of AA along with a doctor named Bob Smith. According to a transcript of one of Bill's AA talks, these are the first principles learned from Ebby:

1. *We admitted we were licked.*

2. *We got honest with ourselves.*

3. *We talked it over with another person.*

4. *We made amends to those we had harmed.*

5. *We tried to carry this message to others with no thought of reward.*

6. *We prayed to whatever God we thought there was.*

Because this "undefined" God later showed up in AA's 12 Steps, many Christians have distanced themselves from the movement. They point out that many use the 12-step recovery as a substitute for faith in Christ and that some 12-step members substitute "the group" for church.

The Need
For Others

It is true that some have seen 12-step recovery groups as more helpful than going to church. People helping people has been an important strength of the 12-step process. The best recovery groups function as compassionate, caring intervention communities of co-strugglers. They share the burden of one another's pain, laugh together, cry together, confront one another, and celebrate together. They expose denial and misbeliefs about their addiction while promoting courage to make tough choices.

Interestingly, these are the kinds of loving relationships called for by the New Testament. Nowhere should principles of recovery and people helping people be more evident than among those of us who believe in Christ and the Bible, from which 12-step recovery was born. What 12-step founders learned from the church some of us now need to learn from recovery groups.

It's also important for us to keep in mind that churches and recovery groups have different purposes. Many churches are not equipped to provide the specific focus and shared need that many 12-step groups provide. At the same time, 12-step groups cannot provide the kind of spiritual family, accountability, and instruction called for by the Bible. They leave God undefined so they can include people of all faiths in the process of overcoming addictions. But recovery groups that define "God as we understood Him" cannot provide all of the spiritual help we need.

◼ TIME OUT FOR THEOLOGY: A Personal God

The Bible teaches that God is not some abstract force or "higher intelligence," but a living, eternal Being.

This is implied in the opening verses of the Bible, which describe God as He created the universe. When He was finished, God said, "It is good," indicating that He was pleased with what He had brought into existence. Only a personal being can experience pleasure!

In addition, God said during creation, "Let Us make man in Our image, according to Our likeness" (Genesis 1:26). It stands to reason that if we are all individual persons, different from any other human being who ever lived, and if we are created in God's image, then He too is a personal being.

—Richard W. De Haan
How To Tell The Truth

3 Breaking the Cycle (Part 1)

STUDY GUIDE
read pages 23-27

To begin to examine the ways a person can find freedom from addiction.

MEMORY VERSE
Romans 6:14—
"For sin shall not have dominion over you, for you are not under law but under grace."

Warming Up

Would you agree that some people are more predisposed to addictions than others? Why or why not?

Thinking Through

1. What is the addictive cycle? What are some things a person can do to try to break this cycle?

2. Explain the concept of "people helping people" espoused in the 12-step recovery process (page 26).

3. Why would you agree or disagree with the authors when they say "some have seen 12-step recovery groups as more helpful than going to church" (page 26)? Do you think that the church has failed to help those with addictions? In what ways has the church helped or not helped those with addictions?

Going Further

Refer

How do these verses provide guidance for getting help from others according to Scripture?

1 Corinthians 12:25

Ephesians 4:2

Ephesians 4:32

1 Thessalonians 4:18

1. What is the value of having a group of fellow believers "bear one another's burdens"? How can that shared burden have a different feel than if you were to share your burden with unbelievers?

2. Verse 5 seems to contrast the "bear one another's burdens" concept when it says, "For each one shall bear his own load." How can those two ideas be reconciled?

3. Verse 7 suggests a standard or principle that relates to the God of the Bible—not to the idea of the undefined God of the 12-step plan. Why is it important to trust the one true God while fighting an addiction?

[1] Brethren, if a man is overtaken in any trespass, you who are spiritual restore such a one in a spirit of gentleness, considering yourself lest you also be tempted. [2] Bear one another's burdens, and so fulfill the law of Christ. [3] For if anyone thinks himself to be something, when he is nothing, he deceives himself. [4] But let each one examine his own work, and then he will have rejoicing in himself alone, and not in another. [5] For each one shall bear his own load.

[6] Let him who is taught the word share in all good things with him who teaches. [7] Do not be deceived, God is not mocked; for whatever a man sows, that he will also reap. [8] For he who sows to his flesh will of the flesh reap corruption, but he who sows to the Spirit will of the Spirit reap everlasting life. [9] And let us not grow weary while doing good, for in due season we shall reap if we do not lose heart. [10] Therefore, as we have opportunity, let us do good to all, especially to those who are of the household of faith.

Prayer Time

Use the *Our Daily Bread* article on the next page as a guide for a devotional and meditation time relating to addictions.

Reflect

1. How would you know when to intervene for a struggling friend or family member—either personally or by suggesting professional help?

2. In what ways have you seen the church—the body of Christ—surround someone in trouble and help him or her?

The Addiction of Us All

There, but for the grace of God, go I." How often I've said that—especially when observing drug-addicted people. I think I say it humbly—but am I really sincere?

In John 8, Jesus told His listeners that His truth could make them free (v. 32). But weren't they free already, they protested? So Jesus tightened the screws a bit more: "Most assuredly, I say to you, whoever commits sin is a slave of sin" (v. 34). In other words, sin is addictive. And since we're all sinners, it's the addiction of us all.

At the heart of every person's sin problem is a "self" habit that can be kicked only through Christ's help. Many recovered drug addicts have found that their "self" habit is a deeper problem than their drug habit. That certainly is Ken's story. After years of running from his problems through drugs and alcohol, he finally yielded his life to Christ. "Since then," Ken testifies, "things haven't always been smooth, but Christ has been transforming my selfish way of life. I was shocked to find that I was completely addicted to me!"

We all battle that same addiction. Instead of flippantly saying, "There, but for the grace of God, go I," we should say, "There go I." No one is an exception. We're all in need of the same grace.

—*Joanie Yoder*

JOHN 8:36—

If the Son makes you free, you shall be free indeed.

■ Read today's
Our Daily Bread at
www.rbc.org/odb

What Does It Take To
Break the
Cycle? PART 2

The Need
For Understanding

Trusting "God as we understood Him" may help people overcome alcohol or drugs, but it doesn't assure forgiveness and a family relationship with God.

Understanding Our God. In the New Testament, the apostle Paul addressed the "undefined God" issue with a group of first-century Athenian philosophers (Acts 17:22–34). While acknowledging that people of all faiths live and move and have their being in God, Paul made it clear that God now calls everyone to accept the One He raised from the dead. Paul was speaking of Jesus, who earlier taught, "God is spirit, and those who worship Him must worship in spirit and truth" (John 4:24).

When we combine these quotes with the rest of the New Testament, we find a God who wants to be known. Even if He helps us overcome an addiction while we are still worshiping "an unknown God," that mercy is not meant to be an end in itself. The God of the Bible gives such mercies to draw us to His full offer of forgiveness, adoption, eternal life, and daily spiritual enablement in Christ.

With that background, let's see how principles for recovery look when seen in the light of a self-revealing God who lovingly reaches out to us in our addiction and sin. This will be difficult for some who have felt criticized and condemned by people who claim to be followers of Christ. But keep in mind that it was Christ himself who earned a reputation as a "friend of sinners."

Jesus didn't die just for His friends. He didn't die just for good people. He died for people like Mary Magdalene, who was possessed by seven demons before being delivered from her enslavement. He died for people captured by their own self-destructive desires for sex, alcohol, and money. That is why the apostle Paul could later write:

> *Do not be deceived. Neither fornicators, nor idolaters, nor adulterers, nor homosexuals, nor sodomites, nor thieves, nor covetous, nor drunkards, nor revilers, nor extortioners will inherit the kingdom of God. And such were some of you. But you were washed, but you were sanctified, but you were justified in the name of the Lord Jesus and by the Spirit of our God (1 Corinthians 6:9–11).*

If these are the kinds of people God declares blameless (justifies), and if these are the kinds of people God sets apart for himself (sanctifies) when they believe in His Son, then there is hope for us as well. God doesn't justify and sanctify good people.

Jesus himself said, "Those who are well have no need of a physician, but those who are sick. I did not come to call the righteous, but sinners, to repentance" (Mark 2:17).

Understanding Our Vulnerability. But don't Christians suffer from addictions? Yes. People can struggle with addictions before and after coming to Christ for forgiveness and eternal salvation. That's one reason Paul had to write to Christians in Corinth (see 1 Corinthians 6:9–11 above). Some were still living under the influence of alcohol and unmanaged sexual desires even after coming to Christ. People bought and owned by God can still struggle with any of the addictions that afflict others. This vulnerability remains as long as we live and groan for relief in these bodies of flesh (Romans 8:23).

But what about those who experience dramatic, lasting deliverance on the day of their salvation? Some do report a "miracle cure" when they first believe in Christ as Lord and Savior. But their story is not the norm. What their experience shows is that God can break the chains of bondage. Their deliverance shows us that God wants His people free to be owned and managed by Him. Their dramatic cures remind all of us that God can empower His people to live under the influence and control of His Spirit.

But dramatic "cold turkey" deliverances are only part of the picture. Even those who experience such freedom in the first days of faith must spend the rest of their lives facing the dangers of countless other enslaving, destructive dependencies. It was to Christians that Paul wrote:

Do not be drunk with wine, in which is dissipation; but be filled with the Spirit, speaking to one another in psalms and hymns and spiritual songs, singing and making melody in your heart to the Lord, giving thanks always for all things to God the Father in the name of our Lord Jesus Christ, submitting to one another in the fear of God (Ephesians 5:18–21).

Here Paul showed that the people of God are not above the danger of addictions. He also showed that Christians have powerful resources for experiencing a new spirituality and healthy dependence on the Spirit of God.

Understanding Our Desires. To understand our addictions, it is important for us to see that our desires are not bad. Our longings for connection, significance, and freedom are given to us by God. What is killing us is the way we are trying to satisfy or deaden those God-given capacities. Addictions are powerful because the desires God made to serve us turn into cruel masters when we allow them to dominate our lives.

Our desire to feel good has a God-given purpose. But when we believe we need relief now, and when our highest priority is to avoid pain, we set ourselves up for an enslaving, destructive dependency. When feeling good or feeling nothing is more important than doing good, loving others, or knowing God, we are ripe for addiction.

Our desires reflect that we have been designed to worship. The philosopher and theologian Augustine was right when he said there is a God-shaped vacuum in all of us, and our hearts are not at rest until we find our rest in Him. If we are not worshiping a good God who loves us, then we will end up worshiping our own desires until they consume us. Addiction becomes an idol.

Our indulged desires, however, do more than consume us. Our desperate efforts to avoid pain inevitably hurt those we love. How can we measure the pain of parents who watch their anorexic daughter starving herself to death? Who can express the pain of a child who grows up with the unpredictability and neglect of an alcoholic parent? Who can describe the anguish of a wife who discovers that her husband has compulsively gambled their marriage into financial bankruptcy?

Yet in spite of the costs to those we love, we still cling to our addictions and insistently deny that we have a problem. Because our desire to feel good or feel nothing seems more important than the truth, denial is a predictable, persistent mark of the person trapped by an enslaving habit.

Self-absorbed desire drives addicted persons to deny they have a problem because they can't imagine living without the object of their dependence. The husband who has been addictively involved in an affair feels far more alive with his lover than he feels with his wife. Alcoholics think they need the bottle to make their lives bearable. Workaholics think they need to work 80 hours a week to prove their importance. It's unthinkable for such persons to give up the source of their good feelings.

When confronted with the damage our addiction and denial does to others, we are likely to blame everyone but ourselves for what is happening. Consumed by our desire to feel good or to feel numb at any cost, we are apt to rage at everyone who confronts us with the truth about ourselves.

Understanding Our Anger. Our anger masks our fear. We rage at heaven and earth because we are afraid to face the light of day. We are terrified at the thought of losing control of the addiction we are using to find relief and control. In our fear, we pursue strategies of "fight" or "flight." We fight everyone who suggests that we have lost control of ourselves and that we are on a path to self-destruction. We flee to the comfort of our "friend" who gives us moments of mind-numbing relief and satisfaction.

Our anger helps to justify our addiction. We believe we deserve the relief our addiction provides. By blaming others for our problems, we keep the focus off ourselves. By blaming God for our pain, we temporarily avoid the issue of our idolatry. As long as we can nurse our complaints against heaven, we don't have to deal with the fact that by our own will, we have chosen gods that allow us to feel good now. As long as we can feel mistreated, neglected, and unloved, we can angrily justify replacing God with our addiction.

In our anger, we forget the One who bore our pain in His own body on an executioner's cross. While blaming others, we do not remember the beatings, the whipping, the scorn, the nails, the thirst, and the tears that were His. As long as we continue to blame God and others for our pain, we ignore the One who absorbed such punishment on our behalf that He himself cried out, "My God, My God, why have You forsaken Me?" (Mark 15:34). By blaming heaven and earth for our problems and numbing ourselves into the mindless comfort of our addictions, we ignore the One who said: "Come to Me, all you who labor and are heavy laden, and I will give you rest" (Matthew 11:28).

4 Breaking the Cycle (Part 2)

To gain an understanding of God and of ourselves as we struggle with addiction.

Warming Up

Do you agree that what those caught in the addictive cycle need most is forgiveness but are often condemned by Christians instead? Why or why not?

Thinking Through

1. How does knowing who God is help us to break the addictive cycle?

2. How do understanding our own vulnerability, our desires, and our anger help us to overcome our addictions?

3. What does it mean for Jesus to be "a friend of sinners"? How can we be a friend to those caught in the addictive cycle?

Going Further

Refer

It is vital when facing struggles to know that God cares. How do these verses help with this idea?

2 Corinthians 1:3–5

Ephesians 2:4

1 Peter 1:3

1. Why did Paul mention the Athenian inscription "TO THE UNKNOWN GOD"? What was he getting at?

22 Then Paul stood in the midst of the Areopagus and said, "Men of Athens, I perceive that in all things you are very religious; 23 for as I was passing through and considering the objects of your worship, I even found an altar with this inscription: TO THE UNKNOWN GOD. Therefore, the One whom you worship without knowing, Him I proclaim to you: 24 God, who made the world and everything in it, since He is Lord of heaven and earth, does not dwell in temples made with hands. 25 Nor is He worshiped with men's hands, as though He needed anything, since He gives to all life, breath, and all things. 26 And He has made from one blood every nation of men to dwell on all the face of the earth, and has determined their preappointed times and the boundaries of their dwellings, 27 so that they should seek the Lord, in the hope that they might grope for Him and find Him, though He is not far from each one of us; 28 for in Him we live and move and have our being, as also some of your own poets have said, . . . 29 "Therefore, since we are the offspring of God, we ought not to think that the Divine Nature is like gold or silver . . . 30 Truly, these times of ignorance God overlooked, but now commands all men everywhere to repent."

2. What characteristics of the one true God did Paul point out in verses 24–27?

3. What is the key element of man's attempt to develop a relationship with God (verse 30)? How does that one decision by us change everything?

Prayer Time

Use the *Our Daily Bread* article on the next page for a devotional time relating to addictions.

Reflect

1. It may be easy to blame God for our problems, but what does Jesus want us to do with our problems instead (Matthew 11:28–30)? How readily do you do this?

2. In what ways does having a personal relationship with God help when you are having a problem such as an addiction?

Victorious Living

A man who drank heavily was converted to Christ and lived victoriously for several weeks. One day as he passed the open door of a bar, the pungent odor aroused his old appetite for liquor. Just then he saw this sign in the window of a nearby cafe: "All the buttermilk you can drink—25 cents!" Dashing inside, he ordered one glass, then another, and still another. After finishing the third, he walked past the saloon and was no longer tempted. He was so full of buttermilk that he had no room for the booze.

Dwight L. Moody once demonstrated the principle of Ephesians 5:18 like this: "Tell me," he said to his audience, "how can I get the air out of the glass I have in my hand?" One man said, "Suck it out with a pump." But the evangelist replied, "That would create a vacuum and shatter it." Finally, after many suggestions, Moody picked up a pitcher and filled the glass with water. "There," he said, "all the air is now removed." He then explained that victory for the child of God does not come by working hard to eliminate sinful habits but rather by allowing the Holy Spirit to take full possession.

Stop trying to "empty yourself" through your will. Instead, study God's Word, confess all known sin, and enjoy by faith the filling with the Spirit. You'll become so occupied with the Savior that there will no longer be room for bad things.

—*Henry Bosch*

EPHESIANS 5:18—

And do not be drunk with wine, in which is dissipation, but be filled with the Spirit.

■ Read today's *Our Daily Bread* at **www.rbc.org/odb**

At the Crossroads

Whether we need forgiveness or spiritual enablement, the God of the Bible makes an offer that asks for our invitation in return. In the Bible, Jesus pictures himself standing at a door knocking, and saying:

> *Behold, I stand at the door and knock. If anyone hears My voice and opens the door, I will come in to him and dine with him, and he with Me (Revelation 3:20).*

At the sound of knocking, we panic or get angry. Our first reaction is apt to be, "Oh no! He's here. The house is a mess. We can't let Him see us like this. If He gets in, He'll make us feel even worse about ourselves than we already feel."

Overwhelmed by fear, we forget that because He is God He already sees us as clearly as if there were no door. He sees every dirty dish, every messy room, every shame, every addiction. He knows everything about us, what kind of shape we're in, and even how angry we are with Him.

In addition to being afraid, we are angry. We are sure He's part of our problem. We don't want to let Him in. He has let us down too many times before. He could have prevented our pain. He could have given us the kind of life He has given others. He hasn't been fair. Yet now He wants more. We sense intuitively that He wants our hearts. He wants to control us. Inviting Him in feels like we're inviting the enemy in.

Yet He knocks. He knows what we find hard to believe. He has come with an offer of relief and comfort and forgiveness and rest. He has come with an offer of enablement. He wants to sit down and eat with us at the table of our heart. He is waiting for our invitation to say something like, "Lord, come in. I've made a mess of things. Please come in and have mercy on me."

When we finally invite Christ into our mess, we discover that He has not come to condemn us. Neither does He demand that we work harder to fix our broken lives. On the contrary, He comes as a loving Savior to the door of our

At this crossroads of invitation, there is an opportunity for change.

hearts, knocking, waiting for us to say, "Yes, Lord, come in. Take over. Forgive me. Change me."

At this crossroads of invitation, there is an opportunity for change. It is an opportunity to discover life through a process of admitting our addiction, acknowledging our pain, accepting responsibility for the damage we've done, pleading for mercy, choosing surrender, and caring for others. Here at this crossroads, our hearts can come alive in the presence of One who—while knowing everything about us—still wants to come into us and be the God and Friend we've been looking for.

Since the thought of beginning this process with God is always frightening, let's take the remaining pages to see what some of the changes might look like if we let Christ into the world of our addictions and sin. In the next few pages, we'll see how surrender and change might look through the eyes of those who have begun the lifetime process of transformation.

Signposts
Of Progress

SIGNPOST #1: WE ADMITTED WE NEEDED HELP.

This first sign of spiritual progress was not easy. The path to freedom and a new life at first felt like death (Matthew 10:39). Admitting to ourselves that we were out of control was hard enough. Confessing the nature of our problem to others felt like insanity. Yet we began to tell our story. By telling others about our struggle, we exposed the truth of our addictions and saw even more clearly that our so-called "friends" were destroying us. Our addictions had robbed us of relationships, dignity, and future.

Once we saw how unmanageable our lives had become, we were ready to depend on the help of God and others to recover the healthy independence and self-control we had lost.

SIGNPOST #2: WE FOUND THAT PAIN WAS NOT OUR ENEMY.

We learned to let sorrow bring us to our senses. Healthy grief allowed us to face the pain our addictions were intended to relieve or kill. Our pain didn't go away. But we found new ways to endure it with courage, hope, and even joy.

We learned to let our pain bring us to the comfort expressed by the author of the 73rd Psalm. He too had been overwhelmed and disillusioned by the unfairness and injustices of life. He couldn't understand how God could let evil people have their way while innocent people like himself suffered. These were painful thoughts. He almost lost his faith. But because he faced his pain and brought it to the place of worship, he suddenly found his heart changed by the perspectives of eternity.

It was too painful for me—until I went into the sanctuary of God;
then I understood their end. Surely You set them in slippery places;
You cast them down to destruction. Oh, how they are brought to desolation,
as in a moment! . . . My heart was grieved, and I was vexed in my mind.
I was so foolish and ignorant; I was like a beast before You.
Nevertheless I am continually with You; You hold me by my right hand.
You will guide me with Your counsel, and afterward receive me to glory.
Whom have I in heaven but You? And there is none upon earth that I desire
besides You. My flesh and my heart fail; but God is the strength of my heart
and my portion forever (Psalm 73:16–19, 21–26).

Like the psalmist, we learned that our pain could bring us to God. We found that our pain did not have to drive us into the arms of our addiction.

SIGNPOST #3: WE LEARNED TO ACCEPT RESPONSIBILITY FOR OUR OWN CHOICES.

We saw evidence that we were overcoming our addiction when we began to see beyond the harm others had done to us.

Instead of merely blaming those who had harmed us, we began seeing how we had chosen to respond to our painful circumstances. Our eyes were opened to the decisions we had been making even in those times when we thought we had no choice but to pursue our addiction. We found motives and choices that bore our signature.

We accepted responsibility for our anger, for the way we tried to satisfy our desires, for demanding relief, for refusing to admit our vulnerability, and for our determination to protect ourselves at all costs, even at the expense of others.

We accepted responsibility for replacing our Creator with an addiction that could not bring light and order to our chaos but instead deepened the darkness in which we were hiding.

At first we were afraid of such responsibility because it increased our sense of failure and loss. We found that we had been as guilty of harming others as they had been guilty of harming us. This deepening awareness, however, turned out for our good. Only when we admitted our wrongs could we find the truth that set us free (John 8:32).

We learned from James, who encouraged us to grieve our sin and to draw near to God (James 4:8–10). And from the apostle Paul we learned that godly sorrow is a healthy road to repentant change (2 Corinthians 7:10).

SIGNPOST #4: **WE SAW OUR NEED FOR MERCY.**

Earlier we had seen our need for help. We had come to believe that only God could free us from the enslavement of our addiction. But then we saw that we needed more than help. We needed mercy. Having seen the many ways we had sinned against God and others, it became clear that we needed undeserved help and forgiveness.

Mercy became our newfound joy. Mercy invited us to a change of heart, a repentance, that would cause us to gladly turn from our idolatrous obsessions. With failure behind us, mercy now called us to a new dependence on God.

When still in the arms of our addiction, the thought of change had seemed like death. Now mercy offered hope and life and freedom. Mercy gave us reason to turn from our futile attempts to find relief and power. Mercy gave us a

For the first time, we had more than momentary pleasure.

new way to look at our God. Mercy's call became stronger than the pull of our addiction. Gradually we saw the One offering mercy as the lover of our souls.

For the first time, we had more than momentary pleasure. Now we had reason to destroy the idol and break all ties with it. Even though we would struggle for the rest of our lives to remember and practice all we had learned, something wonderful had happened. We had been changed. We had tasted joy. In our reflective moments we would always have to admit that the pleasure of our addiction didn't deserve to be compared to the mercies of God.

SIGNPOST #5: **WE DISCOVERED THAT WE HAVE SO MUCH TO BE THANKFUL FOR.**

Only when we discovered the richness of God's mercy did we begin to enjoy the depths of His goodness. We had loved so poorly. We had been so blind. We had so stubbornly insisted on our right to have relief from our pain and have control of our lives. When confronted by those who loved us, we had so persistently denied the truth. Yet seeing this, God still loved us. He forgave us. He even gave us himself in exchange for our brokenness.

With overflowing hearts we clung to the words of David, who wrote, "Blessed is he whose transgression is forgiven, whose sin is covered" (Psalm 32:1). It was when we recognized God's relentless pursuit of us for our good, even in the face of our brazen and idolatrous rebellion against Him, that our hearts were humbled and moved with gratitude for His mercy and grace. From that perspective, we wondered how we could ever have turned our backs on Him for momentary self-destructive pleasures.

Overwhelmed by God's goodness, and having tasted the possibility of being satisfied and complete in Him, we began to find delight in offering ourselves to God as an expression of our worship and love (Romans 12:1).

SIGNPOST #6: **WE DISCOVERED THAT SURRENDER IS A WAY OF LIFE.**

When we first came to the end of ourselves, hit bottom, and admitted that our lives had been shattered, our surrender to God was not complete. In some ways it was a forced surrender. We had been broken by the tyranny of our own choices. The consequences of our resulting enslavement had made our lives unbearable. We finally admitted that we were beaten, and that if we didn't surrender we would die. We surrendered to save our own lives.

What we didn't realize at the time is that this attitude of brokenness could become a way of life. Neither did we realize what a good life it could be. In time, we were surprised by joy. The surrender we feared became a way of inviting the help and mercy of the One who had made us to find our pleasure, security, and fulfillment in Him.

Surrendering our trust in our addiction freed us to depend on the One who always gives far more than He takes. Giving up our self-absorbed goals and resting in Him freed up time and energy that could now be used in serving the needs of others.

SIGNPOST #7: **WE DEVOTED OURSELVES TO HELPING OTHERS.**

While trapped in the chaos of our own addiction, we had nothing but contempt for genuinely intimate relationships. We had so much to hide, and we were so absorbed in our self-protection and relief that we had no energy to spend on anyone but ourselves. But after experiencing the overflowing goodness of God, we found pleasure in leading others to the same supernatural source of freedom. We found that there is no greater expression of gratitude to God than to honor Him by reaching out to others with the restoring love that we received. It was this sense of mission the apostle Paul spoke of when he wrote:

> *Blessed be the God and Father of our Lord Jesus Christ, the Father of mercies and God of all comfort, who comforts us in all our tribulation, that we may be able to comfort those who are in any trouble, with the comfort with which we ourselves are comforted by God (2 Corinthians 1:3–4).*

We discovered that nowhere are people better equipped to help one another than in a church family where individuals see themselves as costrugglers who have so much to be thankful for.

5 At the Crossroads

STUDY GUIDE
read pages 39–45

To begin to see what happens when we make the decision to let Jesus change our lives.

MEMORY VERSE
John 8:36:—
"Therefore if the Son makes you free, you shall be free indeed."

Warming Up

Why is it easier to blame others or even God than to blame ourselves for our addiction?

Thinking Through

1. Why is the prayer "Lord, come in; I have made a mess of things" (page 40), the starting point for recovery from addiction?

2. What are some of the signposts that we are on the way to breaking our addictions?

3. Of the seven signposts discussed (pages 41–45), which is the most meaningful to you? Why?

Going Further

Refer

What is the common theme of these verses, and how does God help us according to these passages?

Luke 4:1–13
1 Corinthians 10:13
Hebrews 2:14–18

1. What does it mean to have your sin "covered" (verse 1)? How does God view the one with covered sin?

> ¹ Blessed is he whose transgression is forgiven, Whose sin is covered. ² Blessed is the man to whom the LORD does not impute iniquity, and in whose spirit there is no deceit. ³ When I kept silent, my bones grew old through my groaning all the day long. ⁴ For day and night Your hand was heavy upon me; My vitality was turned into the drought of summer. Selah. ⁵ I acknowledged my sin to You, and my iniquity I have not hidden. I said, "I will confess my transgressions to the LORD," and You forgave the iniquity of my sin. Selah. ⁶ For this cause everyone who is godly shall pray to You in a time when You may be found; Surely in a flood of great waters they shall not come near him. ⁷ You are my hiding place. You shall preserve me from trouble; You shall surround me with songs of deliverance. Selah.

2. What happens to us if we try to hide our sin or keep from confessing it (verses 3–4)?

3. What could it mean—for someone struggling with a habit that overwhelms—to have the promise of verse 7?

Prayer Time

Use the *Our Daily Bread* article on the next page as a guide for a devotional and meditation time relating to addictions.

Reflect

1. Which of the signposts do you think would be the hardest to accept if you were battling an addiction? Why?

2. When have you been able to help another person who was suffering from an addiction?

Recovering Sinners

People who are trying to become free from an addiction to drugs or alcohol understand an important concept. They know they will always be "recovering."

The lure of those substances is so insidious that former abusers who are wise know how susceptible they are to being sucked in again. They must always be on guard. Time and again we've seen people in the public spotlight who seem to be cured, but who then have a relapse.

That principle is true not only of drug abusers but of all sinners. Those of us who have been redeemed by Jesus Christ's sacrifice on the cross are not recovered sinners, but recovering ones. We are just one sin away from falling back into a self-destructive pattern of behavior. That's why we must be so careful to avoid any activity or relationship that will reintroduce us to the sin we hate.

We are tempted when we are drawn toward a sin. It doesn't become a sin until "desire has conceived" (James 1:15). And the more we deliberately expose ourselves to temptation, the less our resistance will be.

Because we are all recovering sinners, we need to leave plenty of room between us and sin. If we do, we will be less likely to stumble again.

—*Dave Branon*

JAMES 1:21—

Lay aside all filthiness and overflow of wickedness.

■ Read today's *Our Daily Bread* at **www.rbc.org/odb**

Final Thoughts

Rediscovering A Vision Of The Church

W hile the church may not be able to address all of the complicated issues of addiction, it can provide encouragement, understanding, and accountability to those of us caught in its clutches. The church can offer the encouragement of people concerned about our ultimate well-being. It can help us understand our pain in light of both time and eternity. It can help us work through our confused thinking by teaching us to depend on God's Word and the Holy Spirit. It can hold us accountable to live not just for ourselves but also for the interests of others. A healthy church can remind us to pray, work, and watch expectantly for the any-moment return of Christ.

A Look
In The Mirror

It is likely that we all have seen ourselves in the mirror of these pages. What kind of a person have we seen? Have we seen a person who is willing to feel the inevitable and inescapable pains of life? Or have we seen a person committed to relief and control? Have we seen a person vulnerable to addiction because of a refusal to believe that God alone can provide satisfaction and safety?

All of us have the seeds of addiction within ourselves. We all want to minimize our pain. We all want to control our world. At this point, we need to ask ourselves some important questions: "Is there anything in our lives that has become excessive, compulsive, or entangling? Is there anything we feel we cannot let go of because it means too much to us?" If so, we need to be aware that we are ripe for an enslaving, destructive dependency.

The writer of Hebrews warned us that we all need daily encouragement "so that none of [us] may be hardened by sin's deceitfulness" (Hebrews 3:13 NIV). Deception is how addiction gains a foothold. If left unchallenged, deception and denial will spread and blind the heart, resulting in devastating consequences. A man who denies that he has an uncontrolled sexual curiosity is on the edge of developing a fullblown sexual addiction. A man who is unwilling to question the excessive number of hours he spends at work is setting himself up for the relational losses of a workaholic. A woman who refuses to admit that she is using alcohol or food or shopping to change the way she feels is in danger of slipping into the grip of addiction.

If we are walking on the edge, it's time to face the truth. Our hearts are hurting. Our God-given desires are powerful. Our self-absorbed strategies to satisfy those desires will only increase our pain. They will hurt not only us but also those who are closest and dearest to us. Our addictions are gods who have no empathy for us or those we love. It's time for us to hear the loving, pleading voice of God, who says, "Do not be deceived, God is not mocked; for whatever a man sows, that he will also reap. For he who sows to his flesh will of the flesh reap corruption, but he who sows to the Spirit will of the Spirit reap ever-lasting life" (Galatians 6:7–8).

The Pilgrim's Progress

Some enter recovery expecting God to deliver them immediately from their addictive struggles. Few find that to be the case. Most face a long, hard battle with many relapses. But in spite of fallbacks, God doesn't abandon us. Nothing can compare with the process of being forgiven and gradually delivered from self-absorption to self-sacrificing love for the sake of others.

None of us will ever be totally free from our ongoing battle with sin in this life. No matter how far we have progressed, desires will always be found in us that oppose the grace of God. In spite of that fact, God can enable us to live so that we are not irresistibly controlled by God-substitutes that bind us like chains, sap our personal strength, and render us helpless to love Him or others. He can help us to develop a spirit of freedom so that we will be motivated more by the interests of others than by our own immediate pleasure. God can enable us to find in Him a trust and source of life that leads us to gratefully worship Him. When we lose hope in ourselves and in our consuming addictions, He can fill our hearts to overflowing with His amazing grace.

Michael Card captures the beauty of breaking free in his song "Things We Leave Behind." He writes:

> *When we say no*
> *to the things of the world,*
> *we open our hearts*
> *to the love of the Lord;*
> *and it's hard to imagine*
> *the freedom we find*

6 Final Thoughts

To examine our hearts one more time to see if we are ready to tackle the threat of addiction.

Warming Up

If you have an addiction problem, who would you go to for help? Why?

Thinking Through

1. Tim Jackson and Jeff Olson say "all of us have the seeds of addiction within ourselves" (page 50). What do they mean? Why would you agree or disagree?

2. If they are right, what addiction would you be most vulnerable to? What might you do to make sure that you do not succumb to such an addiction?

3. Would you ask your church to help you if you have an addiction problem? Why or why not? What kind of help might you expect the church to give you in your situation?

Going Further

Refer

Thoughts for pilgrims: As we move along in our lives toward Christlikeness, how do these verses encourage us?

1. Hebrews 13:5
2. 1 John 1:9
3. Romans 12:2
4. Romans 6:18

Digging In   Read   James 1:13–18

1. Verse 14 gives a pattern for the progress of sin in a life. How does this verse and the idea given by the writers of "walking on the edge" provide us a warning that could keep us out of trouble?

> [13] Let no one say when he is tempted, "I am tempted by God"; for God cannot be tempted by evil, nor does He Himself tempt anyone. [14] But each one is tempted when he is drawn away by his own desires and enticed. [15] Then, when desire has conceived, it gives birth to sin; and sin, when it is full-grown, brings forth death. [16] Do not be deceived, my beloved brethren. [17] Every good gift and every perfect gift is from above, and comes down from the Father of lights, with whom there is no variation or shadow of turning. [18] Of His own will He brought us forth by the word of truth, that we might be a kind of firstfruits of His creatures.

2. If we want what is good in life, according to verse 17, what should we look to for our source? How is this different from looking to what can be addictive?

3. It seems that God has a design for our lives (verse 18) that could help us want to avoid trouble. What is that design?

Prayer Time

Use the *Our Daily Bread* article on the next page as a guide for a devotional and meditation time relating to addictions.

Reflect

1. How would I characterize what I know now about addictions that I didn't know before?

2. What are some things that I am determined to leave behind lest they trip me up?

Free To Come Back

When I first acquired an adorable puppy named Dolly, she filled my days with frequent trips to my backyard. Then she began using these occasions to explore places I didn't want her to go. By offering her a reward, I was able to teach her to respond to my command, "Come!" But eventually, the rewards weren't enough to get her to come back to me. So I bought a leash on a reel that gives Dolly a safe amount of freedom, but gives me the option of "reeling her in" when she ventures too far.

PSALM 31:22 —

I said in my haste, "I am cut off from before Your eyes."

This reminds me of how God rescued a drug-addicted man named Derek. Longing to break his addiction, he stayed in our home, where he became God's child. He overcame his habit but he still battled with temptation. One day he gave in, ran away, and used some drugs. Then guilt overwhelmed him as he sat despondently on a park bench. He felt like the psalmist David (Psalm 31:22) and said to himself, "I'm cut off from the Lord. I'm finished." But the long leash of God's love tugged on his heart. Immediately, Derek asked for the Lord's forgiveness and made his way back to us (32:3–5).

If you're going the wrong way and feel cut off from God, remember, you can return. Respond to the tug of His forgiving love on your heart and come back to Him today.

—*Joanie Yoder*

■ Read today's *Our Daily Bread* at **www.rbc.org/odb**

54

SUGGESTED RESOURCES

Addiction And Grace: Love And Spirituality In The Healing Of Addictions
by Gerald May (HarperOne, 2006).

Don't Call It Love: Recovery From Sexual Addiction
by Patrick Carnes (Bantam Books, 1992).

False Intimacy: Understanding The Struggle Of Sexual Addiction
by Harry W. Schaumburg (NavPress, 1997).

Shattered Dreams
by Larry Crabb (Waterbrook Press, 2001).

The Healing Path
by Dan Allender (Waterbrook Press, 2000).

The Last Addiction: Why Self-Help Is Not Enough
by Sharon Hersh (WaterBrook Press, 2008).

The Truth About Addiction And Recovery
by Stanton Peele with Archie Brodsky (Fireside, 1992).

Twelve Steps And Twelve Traditions
by Alcoholics Anonymous World Services, Inc. (Hazelden
Information Education, 1996).

OTHER RELATED RBC COUNSELING BOOKLETS

Designed For Desire—*God's design for sexuality* (CB932).

When A Man's Eye Wanders—breaking the power of pornography (CB991).

When Help Is Needed—a biblical view of counseling (CB931).

LEADER'S and USER'S GUIDE

Overview of Lessons

Pulpit Sermon Series (for pastors and church leaders)

Although the Discovery Series Bible Study is primarily for personal and group study, pastors may want to use this material as the foundation for a series of messages on this important issue. The suggested topics and their corresponding texts from the Overview of Lessons above can be used as an outline for a sermon series.

DSBS User's Guide (for individuals and small groups)

Individuals—Personal Study

• Read the designated pages of the book.

• Carefully consider the study questions, and write out answers for each.

Small Groups—Bible-Study Discussion

• To maximize the value of the time spent together, each member should do the lesson work prior to the group meeting.

• Recommended discussion time: 45 minutes.

• Engage the group in a discussion of the questions—seeking full participation from each member.

Note To The Reader

The publisher invites you to share your reponse
to the message of this book by writing
Discovery House Publishers, P.O. Box 3566,
Grand Rapids, MI 49501, USA. For information
about other Discovery House books, music,
videos, or DVDs, contact us at the same
address or call 1-800-653-8333. Find us on the
Internet at **http://www.dhp.org/** or send e-mail
to **books@dhp.org**.